Fish recipes

FROM THE SOUTH-WEST

HEATHER CORBETT

D0865420

TOR MARK • REDRUTH

Other books in the Tor Mark series

Ancient Cornwall
Birds of Cornwall
Birds of Devon
Charlestown
China clay
Classic Cornish ghost stories
Classic Devon ghost stories
Classic folk tales from the
Land's End
Classic ghost stories from the
Land's End
Classic West Country ghost stories
Clotted cream
Colour beneath the sea
Cornish cheeses
Cornish fairies
Cornish folklore
Cornish inventors
Cornish legends
Cornish mining – underground
Cornish mining industry
Cornish recipes
Cornish saints
Cornish seashore
Cornish smuggling industry
Cornwall's engine houses
Cornwall's history – an introduction
Cornwall's industrial past

Cornwall's railways
Devon customs and superstitions
Devon legends
Devon seashore
Devonshire jokes and stories
Do you know Cornwall?
Jan Bedella's fiddle
Lost ports of Cornwall
New Cornish cookbook
The pasty book
Shipwrecks around Land's End
Shipwrecks around the Lizard
Shipwrecks of North Devon
Shipwrecks on Cornwall's North
coast
The story of the Cornish language
The story of St Ives
The story of Truro Cathedral
Strange tales of the Cornish coast
Tales of the Cornish smugglers
Twelve walks on the Lizard
Wildflowers of the Cornish coast
Wildflowers of the Devon coast
Wildflowers of the Cornish
hedgerows
Wildflowers of the Devon
hedgerows

Acknowledgements

Thanks are due for the expertise and knowledge of the following firms,
whose web sites you may find useful (see page 48): The Pilchard Works,
Newlyn; Matthew Stevens of M Stevens & Son, fishmongers of St Ives;
Cornish Cuisine, Penryn. The cover photograph is by Andrew Besley,
with the kind cooperation of M Stevens & Son.

Published by Tor Mark, PO Box 4 Redruth, Cornwall TR16 5YX
ISBN 0-85025-401-9
Printed in Great Britain by Cornwall Litho, Redruth

Contents

Introduction

Fish is the original fast food – in earlier times cooked quickly over a fire or baked in the embers.

In the past many were put off cooking fish because of the difficulty of preparation; cookery books used to be full of drawings on how to fillet fish – wonderful if you can do it, but exasperating if you're unsure. These days fish requires little preparation, and fishmongers are very user-friendly – they are keen to sell fish and so will fillet and prepare it, and many of them will even suggest how to cook it. All you have to do is go home and follow their advice. I have had lots of good recipes from fishmongers over the years.

Nearly all the recipes in this book are cooked in a hot oven. This has a double advantage – the smell does not get out, and the fish is cooked very fast in one dish. Once it's in the oven you just have time to take a sip from a glass of wine and 'hey presto' your dinner is ready!

The recipes aim to be easy, fast, successful and interesting. I have cooked – and adapted them – over the years for family and friends. Fish cookery is far more enticing and exciting than it used to be. Forget those childhood memories of nauseous fishy smells and a mouthful of bones – fish cooking has grown up and is the ultimate quality food in this busy world.

Above all, fish is good for you! It does not have the calories of meat, yet it has a similar vitamin content. Oily fish like mackerel, herring and sardines have the added bonus of reducing the possibility of heart disease and strokes.

The fish used in these recipes are those caught all around the coast of the South-west and sold at the fish markets of Newlyn, Padstow, Looe, Plymouth and Brixham. Much from these markets goes 'up country' or, sadly, is exported to Europe – Spain and

France buy a good deal of British fish and in both countries restaurants around the coast have a reputation for cooking 'local' fish!

Newlyn, with its working harbour, has the second largest fishing fleet in Britain. You can walk along the quay, look at the fishing boats and see the fish market – but don't get in the way! Most of the boats are beam trawlers. They have a crew of five and fish up to 100 miles out, in winds often reaching gale force, for seven days at a time before returning home for a few days. It is a hard and dangerous life.

Most of the varieties of fish caught in the West Country are available throughout Britain in local fishmongers and at supermarket fish stalls. Whenever possible buy fish that is fresh, rather than frozen, and cook it quickly – that way the fish will have an incomparable taste. It's best to shop with an open mind – go for what looks good on the day and adapt your recipe accordingly.

Many of the recipes in this book are interchangeable – if you haven't got all the ingredients, be confident, substitute. Above all, be inventive and enjoy the results!

Cod with Coriander and Saffron

This is an unusual treatment of cod, which makes a change from the run-of-the-mill recipes, and is a very pretty dish. When cod is not available this dish would work well with grey mullet or pollack.

For 4

4 x 150 g / 5 oz pieces of cod fillet
1 teaspoon crushed green peppercorns
1 teaspoon crushed coriander seeds
12 strands of saffron
225 ml / 8 fl oz white wine
110 ml / 4 fl oz olive oil
12 cherry tomatoes
1 tablespoon chopped parsley
1 tablespoon balsamic vinegar

Bring the white wine to the boil and pour over the roughly chopped green peppercorns, coriander seeds and saffron. Pour a little of the olive oil into an ovenproof dish, lay in the 4 pieces of cod and the cherry tomatoes. Cover with the saffron and white wine mix, and add a little more olive oil.

Cook in a hot oven 230°C / 450°F / gas mark 8 for about 15 minutes. Before serving, add the balsamic vinegar and the parsley. Serve with plain rice or couscous.

Cod Fillets
with Cucumber, Spring Onions
and Cream

Cooked cucumber may seem odd but it adds a wonderful colour and texture to the dish. Sadly not much cod will be caught around our shores for a few years because of EC restrictions, although I am told on good authority that there are always plenty two miles off Newlyn in the spring.

For 4

450 g / 1 lb cod fillets
4 spring onions finely chopped
10 cm / 4 inches cucumber roughly chopped
olive oil
1 glass white wine
200 ml / 7 fl oz double cream
$^1/_2$ tablespoon chopped dill or parsley

Drizzle a little olive oil onto the base of an ovenproof dish and place the cod fillets, cut into large pieces, on top. Place the spring onions and cucumber on top of the fish and then add the white wine.

Bake in a hot oven 230°C / 450°F / gas mark 8 for about 15 minutes, depending on the thickness of the fish. Add the cream and the dill or parsley, and return to the oven to heat through. This dish is good with new potatoes and French beans.

Cod with Runner Beans

This is a surprising and wonderful dish based on a Jamie Oliver recipe that I found in a newspaper. The runner beans could be replaced by French beans.

For 4

4 x 110-175 g / 4-6 oz pieces of cod fillet
4 slices smoked bacon
450 g / 1 lb runner beans thinly sliced
12 cherry tomatoes
12 black olives
olive oil
2 lemons halved
1 tablespoon chopped parsley or chives

Place the beans, cherry tomatoes, lemons and olives in a lightly oiled ovenproof dish. Wrap the slices of bacon around each piece of cod, place amongst the beans and then drizzle with a little olive oil.

Cook in a hot oven 230°C / 450°F / gas mark 8 for about 15 minutes, depending on the size of the cod. Decorate with the chopped parsley or chives. This dish goes well with plain rice or couscous.

Fish Crumble

Any fish will do for this homely dish, although it's nice to get a range of textures – a little cooked salmon adds a lovely colour as well as texture and flavour.

For 4

450 g / 1 lb assorted white fish (see above)
20 cooked prawns (defrosted if using frozen prawns)
2 hardboiled eggs roughly chopped
1 tablespoon chopped parsley
4 spring onions chopped

For the crumble
40 g / 1^1/$_2$ oz butter
75 g / 3 oz plain flour
50 g / 2 oz Cheddar cheese grated

For the sauce to bind
40 g / 1^1/$_2$ oz butter
40 g / 1^1/$_2$ oz plain flour
250 ml / 8 fl oz milk
125 ml / 4 fl oz cider or white wine
coarse sea salt and ground black pepper to taste

Make the crumble by rubbing the butter into the flour to form breadcrumbs and then adding the cheese. Make the sauce by melting the butter in a saucepan, mixing in the flour and allowing the two to cook for a moment. Add the milk and the cider or wine very slowly indeed – being too enthusiastic here will cause the sauce to go lumpy. Season with salt and pepper to taste.

Place all the fish, prawns, egg, parsley and spring onions into an ovenproof dish and pour the sauce over. Top with the crumble mix and cook in a hot oven 230°C / 450°F / gas mark 8 for 15-20 minutes until cooked through.

Red Gurnard Fillets with Celery and Apple

Gurnard needs to be well filleted, as small pinbones left in can be very irksome. It has a good flavour and is quite firm. The skin is a beautiful pinky red which looks very pretty peeping through the sauce. It is available all the year round.

For 4

4 red gurnard filleted
3 sticks of celery sliced thinly
2 apples chopped into small chunks
4 spring onions chopped
25 g / 1 oz butter
275 ml / 10 fl oz single cream
1 tablespoon French flat leaf parsley chopped
1 tablespoon chopped walnuts for decoration

Butter an ovenproof dish. Place in it the gurnard fillets, and sprinkle the celery, apple and spring onions on top. Pour over the single cream, cover with tinfoil and put in a hot oven 230°C / 450°F / gas mark 8.

Cook for 10 minutes, uncover and cook for a further 5 minutes. Decorate with the parsley and the walnuts. Serve with broccoli and mashed potatoes sprinkled with some more French parsley.

Smoked Haddock and Mushroom Lasagne

Surprisingly, fish makes good lasagne – shellfish can also be used successfully.

For 4

450 g / 1 lb smoked haddock fillets, cooked and flaked
1 onion roughly chopped
110 g / 4 oz mushrooms chopped
1 x 400 g / 14 oz tin chopped tomatoes
paprika
coarse sea salt and ground black pepper to taste
1 tablespoon chopped parsley
olive oil
9 sheets egg lasagne – the sort that does not require pre-cooking
275 ml / 10 fl oz plain yoghurt
1 egg
4 tablespoons grated Parmesan

Fry the onion and the mushrooms in a little oil to soften. Add the tinned tomatoes, a large pinch of paprika and sea salt and ground black pepper to taste, and cook for 5 minutes.

In an oiled ovenproof dish place a third of the smoked haddock, followed by a third of the tomato sauce mixture. Place 3 sheets of lasagne on top. Repeat twice more. Mix the yoghurt, egg and 3 tablespoons Parmesan together and spread over the last layer of lasagne. Sprinkle the remaining Parmesan on top.

Bake in a medium oven 180°C / 350°F / gas mark 4 for 25 minutes or until cooked. Serve decorated with the parsley.

Smoked Haddock and Spinach Tart

Smoked fish and spinach seem to be natural companions and in a tart the mix of colours is delightful.

For 4

For the pastry
110 g/4 oz plain flour
50 g/2 oz butter
water to mix

For the filling
450 g/1 lb spinach cooked, well drained and chopped
225 g/8 oz smoked haddock, cooked and flaked
2 tomatoes
3 eggs
275 ml/10 fl oz milk
150 ml/5 fl oz double cream
1 tablespoon grated Parmesan
1 tablespoon parsley chopped
coarse sea salt and ground black pepper

Make the pastry in the usual way, rubbing the fat into the flour and adding the water to mix – place in the fridge to keep cool. Whisk the eggs with the milk, cream and the parsley, and season to taste with coarse sea salt and ground black pepper.

Roll out the pastry and place in a 20 cm/8 inch flan dish. Add the spinach and the haddock, and pour over the egg mix to cover. Slice the tomatoes and arrange decoratively on top, and sprinkle with Parmesan. Bake at 180°C/350°F/gas mark 4 for 35-40 minutes until cooked.

Spanish Hake

Much of the hake caught in our waters is exported to Spain, where it is highly valued. If you are lucky enough to find some hake in your fishmonger's, do not hesitate to buy it – it has enough character to be combined with strong Mediterranean flavours. This recipe is based on one found in Spain on holiday. It was so good, I had to import it!

For 4

4 x 110g/4oz pieces of hake
50g/2oz chorizo sausage chopped into small cubes
1 large onion chopped
2 medium courgettes sliced thinly
1 x 400g/14oz tin chopped tomatoes
olive oil
150ml/5floz sherry
$1/4$ teaspoon paprika
1 lemon sliced into wedges
sea salt and ground black pepper to taste

First fry the chopped onion and the chorizo together. When softened, place in the bottom of an ovenproof dish. Add the 4 pieces of hake, and cover them with the thin slices of courgette and the paprika. Mix the chopped tomato and the sherry, add a little salt and pepper, and pour over the assembled ingredients.

Place in a hot oven 230°C/450°F/gas mark 8 for 20 minutes. Serve with plain boiled rice and lemon wedges.

Hake Steaks with Lemon and Green Olives

Cod steaks are very difficult to find these days, but hake is a good substitute.

For 4

4 x 110g/4oz hake steaks
juice of 1 lemon
2 tablespoons olive oil and a little more
1 tablespoon chopped parsley
2 cloves garlic chopped
4 tablespoons breadcrumbs
coarse sea salt and ground black pepper
12 green olives pitted and roughly chopped

First marinade the hake steaks in the lemon juice and olive oil for at least an hour – but longer is better, if you can remember. Mix the breadcrumbs, parsley, salt, pepper and garlic.

Place the fish in an ovenproof dish with the marinade – sprinkle the breadcrumb topping over the fish and place in a hot oven 230°C/450°F/gas mark 8 for 20 minutes. Decorate with the olives before serving. Rice goes well with this dish.

Peppered Herring

Herring is around for much of the year, is readily available and is reasonably versatile. It has quite a strong flavour and a creamy texture. One of the most successful recipes is herring dipped in oatmeal – here is an interesting variation.

For 4

4 herrings filleted
olive oil
1 tablespoon black peppercorns
1 tablespoon flour
balsamic vinegar (if liked)

Crush the black peppercorns in a mortar and pestle or in a polythene bag with a rolling pin, mix with the flour and spread out on a large plate. Roll the herrings on both sides in the mixture and place in an oiled ovenproof dish. Sprinkle a little olive oil over the top and bake in a hot oven 230°C/450°F/gas mark 8 for 10 minutes.

Serve with a very little balsamic vinegar sprinkled on top. A robust red wine, French bread and French beans are excellent with this dish.

Red Fillets of John Dory

John Dory is an unusual fish with a good texture which flakes slightly when cut with a knife – it is firm so that the fillets hold their shape when cooked. It is available for much of the year.

For 4

2 John Dory filleted
16 cherry tomatoes
1 red pepper thinly sliced
olive oil
juice of half a lemon
4 spring onions finely chopped
$1/2$ tablespoon chopped parsley
small pinch of paprika

Pour a small quantity of olive oil in an ovenproof dish, and place the John Dory fillets, cut in half lengthways for easier serving, on top.

Add the red pepper, cherry tomatoes, lemon juice and paprika, cover with tin foil and place in a hot oven 230°C/450°F/gas mark 8 for about 15 minutes. Uncover and add the spring onions and parsley.

This is very good served with a small quantity of mushroom and herb risotto.

Grey Mullet with Roasted Vegetables and Avocado Raita

Although the name grey mullet does not sound very enticing, it is a fine fish – quite firm and robust. They can be a good size so that one fish between two may be ample – you will need to decide this yourself.

For 4

2 grey mullet filleted
1 red pepper sliced into chunks
2 medium courgettes chopped roughly
2 small red onions roughly chopped
2 sprigs of thyme
1 ripe avocado chopped into small cubes
275 ml / 10 fl oz natural yoghurt
1/4 teaspoon paprika
3 tablespoons olive oil
coarse sea salt and ground black pepper

Place the vegetables in an ovenproof dish with 2 tablespoons of the olive oil. Add the sprigs of thyme and a little salt and pepper. Roast in a hot oven 230°C / 450°F / gas mark 8 for 20 minutes.

Remove from the oven; place the grey mullet fillets on top, flesh side up. Drizzle the remainder of the olive oil over the fish and return to the oven for a further 10 minutes or until the fish is cooked.

While the fish is cooking, make the avocado raita by combining the yoghurt and the chopped avocado. Sprinkle a little paprika on the top as decoration. This raita should be offered with the fish, rather than being poured over it. New potatoes go well with this dish.

White Fish with Brie

This is a very useful way of using up any left over cooked white fish – cod, pollack, mullet, monkfish, plaice, sole… anything will be fine. The recipe is so good it is worth cooking fish especially for it – simply bring the fish to the boil in a saucepan and then leave to cool. Sorry, this will make a fishy smell, so open the window or close the kitchen door!

For 4

450 g/1 lb cooked white fish
175 g/6 oz mushrooms thinly sliced
2 cloves of garlic crushed
2 tablespoons chopped chives and/or parsley
ground black pepper
225 g/8 oz Brie
butter

Flake the cooked fish into bite-sized chunks. Butter an ovenproof serving dish and place the fish in it in one layer. The finely sliced mushrooms are placed on top of this with a little ground black pepper, 1 tablespoon of the herbs and the crushed garlic. Finally add a layer of Brie, which has been cut into 6 mm/1/4 inch slices – do not cut off the rind, as it gives an interesting chewy texture.

Place in a hot oven 230°C/450°F/gas mark 8 for 15 minutes when the Brie should be wonderfully runny. Decorate with the remainder of the chopped herbs. New potatoes and peas or French beans go nicely with this dish.

Baked Mackerel
with Cider, Orange and Chives

Fresh mackerel is a beautiful fish to look at – silver and blue green. It is essential that it is eaten as fresh as possible – it does not keep well: this is why so much is smoked (the best mackerel for smoking are those caught during the winter months from November to March, as they are much more oily). Increasingly mackerel in the South-west are line caught – these are the ones you should buy to ensure that mackerel fishing is sustainable. The orange in this recipe cuts through the oiliness of the fish.

For 4

4 mackerel fillets
150 ml / 5 fl oz cider
2 oranges
4 spring onions chopped
olive oil
coarse sea salt and ground black pepper

Grate the orange rind, peel the oranges and cut into slices. Place half the orange slices on the base of an ovenproof dish, arrange the mackerel fillets on top, place the remainder of the orange slices over the fish, and then sprinkle the orange rind and the spring onion on top. Pour the cider over the fish and season to taste.

Put in a hot oven 230°C / 450°F / gas mark 8 for 10-15 minutes until cooked. Serve with French bread and a salad.

Smoked Mackerel Instant Pasta

In Cornwall and Devon there are a number of small firms smoking not only mackerel, haddock and cod but all sorts of fish and meats. One national award-winning business that does mail order is Cornish Cuisine of Penryn.

Smoked mackerel adds a distinctive flavour to old favourites, such as cauliflower cheese or macaroni cheese. Simply flake the smoked mackerel fillets and add to the cheese sauce.

For 4

4 smoked mackerel fillets flaked
450 g / 1 lb fresh pasta
570 ml / 1 pt single cream
1 tablespoon grated Parmesan
4 spring onions roughly chopped
225 g / 8 oz mushrooms roughly chopped
butter
salt and ground black pepper to taste
1 tablespoon chopped parsley

Cook the mushrooms and spring onions in the melted butter in a saucepan for 5 minutes over a medium heat until softened. Add the flaked smoked mackerel and heat through, and then add the cream, making sure that you do not allow it to boil.

Cook the fresh pasta as directed on the packet, place in a serving dish, add the mackerel mix and the grated Parmesan, and mix together lightly. Sprinkle with the chopped parsley and ground black pepper to taste.

Smoked Mackerel, Potatoes and Leeks

Smoked mackerel is a useful store cupboard fish, as it keeps for some time vacuum-packed in the fridge or even longer in the freezer.

This is a truly classic dish and can be varied in a number of ways very effectively.

For 4

4 small smoked mackerel fillets
2 medium leeks cut across into 5mm/¼ in slices
275 ml/10 fl oz single cream
200 ml/7 fl oz milk
1 tablespoon grain mustard or horseradish sauce
450 g/1 lb potatoes, peeled and cut into 5 mm/¼ in slices
butter
salt and ground black pepper to taste

Butter an ovenproof dish. Place in it a layer of potatoes, then leeks, then flaked smoked mackerel. Repeat this and finish with a layer of potato.

Mix together the cream, milk and mustard or horseradish. Carefully pour this over the top so that it goes through the layers, adding ground black pepper to taste. Cover with tin foil and put in a hot oven 230°C/450°F/gas mark 8 for about 50 minutes.

Test the middle of the dish with a skewer to see if the potato is cooked – when this is the case, remove the tin foil and cook for another 10 minutes to brown the potatoes on top.

Smoked Mackerel Salad

This seems to appear on nearly every pub menu and yet it is not as exciting as it could be – it should not be a few salad 'trimmings', but a real salad in which the smoked mackerel has a particular part to play.

For 4

For the salad
225 g/8 oz cooked new potatoes, cubed if too large
3 sticks celery sliced
4 spring onions roughly chopped
1 large bunch of watercress
1 green crisp apple chopped
2 smoked mackerel fillets in large chunks
2 tablespoons seedless green grapes
2 tablespoons green olives
1 tablespoon chopped coriander
1 avocado roughly sliced
1 tablespoon sunflower seeds

For the lemon dressing
4 tablespoons olive oil
1 tablespoon freshly squeezed lemon juice
$1/4$ teaspoon English mustard powder
$1/4$ teaspoon caster sugar
sea salt and ground black pepper to taste

To make the dressing, mix the mustard powder and the sugar together, add the olive oil and stir well. Then add the lemon juice and the salt and pepper. Place the watercress in a salad bowl and arrange the other ingredients on top of it. Top with the dressing and leave for 10 minutes for the flavours to develop.

Monkfish and Bacon

This is a traditional French recipe which is always a surprise when brought to the table. Monkfish is a versatile fish, as it can be used in a number of ways – either in large pieces which are 'carved' as here or in smaller pieces for a risotto. It is available all year round. The recipe for tuna stew (page 40) or squid with garlic, coriander and olives (page 37) would do very well with monkfish.

For 4

700 g / 1½ lb monkfish tail in a piece
4-6 rashers of smoked bacon
8 sage leaves
2 cloves garlic crushed
olive oil
balsamic vinegar or lemon juice

Firstly make sure that the fishmonger has taken the central bone out of the monkfish and cleaned off all the skin. The fish should still be more or less in one piece.

Place the sage leaves and the garlic along the length of the fish and then wrap the bacon rashers around it. Put in an oiled roasting pan and drizzle a little olive oil over it. Place in a hot oven 230°C/450°F/gas mark 8 for 30 minutes.

Arrange on a serving dish and drizzle a little balsamic vinegar or lemon juice over. The fish should be served in slices about 4 cm / 1½ inch thick. This dish would be very good with thickly cut sauté potatoes and a green salad.

Monkfish Risotto with Saffron

Monkfish, tuna, shellfish and squid all lend themselves to being made into risotto.

For 4

450g/1lb monkfish fillet cut into bite-size chunks
1 onion chopped
2 green peppers chopped
2 cloves garlic crushed
12 saffron threads
$^1/_2$ teaspoon paprika
225g/8oz Arborio risotto rice
1 glass white wine, vermouth or sherry
425ml/15floz fish or vegetable stock
1 tablespoon French parsley chopped
a few (defrosted) cooked prawns for decoration
lemon wedges
coarse sea salt and ground black pepper to taste
olive oil

Fry the monkfish pieces in oil in a large frying pan or paella pan until they are nearly cooked. Remove and set aside. Fry the onion, garlic and the peppers gently until soft, then add the rice, stirring so that all the grains are covered with oil. Cover with the hot stock in which you have infused the saffron, and add the wine, vermouth or sherry, paprika and salt and pepper. Leave on a medium heat to cook – do not stir.

After 10 minutes return the monkfish to the pan, pushing it down in amongst the rice. Continue to simmer until the rice is cooked and the liquid more or less evaporated. If the rice is not cooked but is dry, add a little more liquid – water or wine – and continue to cook.

Decorate with prawns, lemon wedges and parsley.

Orange and Salt Pilchard Salad

Salacche salate Inglesi have long been made in Newlyn and exported to Italy. The pilchards are salted and pressed and preserved in barrels. You can see the process at the Pilchard Works, Newlyn, which is open as a working museum. The pilchards are available in England in jars with olive oil or sunflower oil and are sold in some supermarkets. The taste is very similar to anchovy and the fish can be used in the same way.

This recipe is based upon one suggested by the Pilchard Works. It comes from an Italian mountain village near Sasso Marconi, which is twinned with Helston in Cornwall.

For 4

2 large oranges
8 salt pilchard fillets chopped
3 tablespoons olive oil
1 teaspoon fresh basil chopped
1 teaspoon fresh parsley chopped
$1/2$ lemon squeezed
ground black pepper
12 black olives
assorted salad leaves or lettuce

Peel the oranges carefully, removing as much pith as you can, then slice into wedges. In a bowl mix the salted pilchards, olive oil, herbs, lemon juice and ground black pepper to taste.

Place in the fridge for at least 1 hour to allow the flavours to merge. Serve on a bed of salad leaves or lettuce decorated with the black olives.

Marinaded Salt Pilchards

Marinading salt pilchards is a good idea – it means that you always have something interesting waiting in the fridge which needs no cooking at all. Marinaded salt pilchards will keep in the fridge for at least five days.

For 4

8 filleted salt pilchards

Red onion and sun-dried tomato marinade
3 tablespoons olive oil
2 garlic cloves roughly chopped
1 sprig thyme
2 bay leaves
$1/2$ lemon squeezed
4 sun-dried tomatoes
$1/2$ red onion thinly sliced
ground black pepper to taste

Green pepper and orange marinade
3 tablespoons olive oil
2 garlic cloves roughly chopped
1 tablespoon cider vinegar
$1/2$ onion thinly sliced
1 small green pepper thinly sliced
1 tablespoon drained capers
$1/2$ small orange thinly sliced
ground black pepper to taste

Place the salt pilchard fillets in a dish, mix the marinade ingredients together and pour over them. Cover with clingfilm and place in the fridge for up to 5 days, so that the flavours mingle. Sprinkle with chopped herbs of your choice. Serve with warm crusty bread.

Spaghetti with Salt Pilchard Puttanesca

This is based on a traditional Italian recipe found by the Pilchard Works, which uses salt pilchards, although you frequently find it in English recipe books with anchovies. Use the salt pilchards and you are being genuinely Italian.

Look out for the Pilchard Works tinned pilchard fillets in olive oil, following a traditional method of 1820/30, where the fillets are flash fried before being tinned by hand.

For 4

350 g/12 oz dried spaghetti
1 x 400 g/14 oz tin chopped tomatoes
1 tablespoon olive oil
4 salt pilchards chopped into small pieces
2 cloves garlic thinly sliced
16 black olives stoned and sliced
1 tablespoon drained capers
1 tablespoon parsley chopped
ground black pepper to taste

Put the spaghetti on to cook.

Fry the tomatoes in a little oil for 3 minutes. Add the rest of the ingredients and cook for another 3 minutes. When the spaghetti is cooked, drain and put into a serving dish. Pour the sauce over it. Serve with fresh grated Parmesan cheese.

West Country Plaice

Plaice is a moist, delicate fish, so it is important not to overwhelm it with strong flavoured ingredients. The addition of cider and Cheddar cheese gives a West Country interest while the tomato adds colour. Plaice is at its best from May to December.

For 4

225 g/8 oz chopped onion or leeks (which are prettier)
4 plaice fillets
2 tomatoes thinly sliced
150 ml/5 fl oz dry cider
50 g/2 oz Cheddar cheese grated
butter
1 tablespoon dill chopped
sea salt and ground black pepper to taste

Fry the onion or leek in butter until softened and then put in an ovenproof dish. Place the four plaice fillets on the onion/leek, and put the sliced tomato on top. Sprinkle the cheese and most of the dill over the fish, add sea salt and ground black pepper to taste, and drizzle the cider into the dish.

Place in a hot oven 230°C/450°F/gas mark 8 for about 10 minutes before serving. Decorate with the remaining dill.

Plaice with Garlic Mushrooms

Garlic mushrooms are a very popular starter. Here they make plaice into a luscious main course.

For 4

4 small or 2 large plaice filleted
4 cloves garlic chopped
225 g/8 oz mushrooms finely chopped
50 g/2 oz butter
1 tablespoon parsley finely chopped
150 ml/5 fl oz white wine
1 lemon cut into curls or wedges
sea salt and ground black pepper to taste

Soften the butter and beat into it the chopped garlic, parsley and mushrooms. If the plaice are large, cut the fillets in half lengthways. Pour a little of the white wine into an ovenproof dish, place half the fillets into the dish, spread the mushroom mixture over them and then place the other fillets on top, making a kind of sandwich. Add sea salt and ground black pepper to taste. Cover with the remainder of the wine.

Put in a hot oven 230°C/450°F/gas mark 8 for 15-20 minutes depending on the thickness of the plaice – check after 15 to be on the safe side. Decorate with the lemon which takes away some of the richness of the buttery sauce.

Pollack with Mayonnaise and Yoghurt

For years pollack has been ignored as a cheap fish and so much of it is exported to Brittany, but now that cod is expensive and less readily available it is coming into its own. The fillets are usually a good size and therefore can be cut into customised portions. It is best from August to March. Mayonnaise and yoghurt seems an odd combination but it makes a very pleasant sauce.

For 4

4 portions of pollack fillet
4 spring onions chopped
4 tablespoons mayonnaise
4 tablespoons plain yoghurt
4 tablespoons breadcrumbs
butter
$1/4$ teaspoon paprika
$1/2$ glass white wine for marinade

First marinade the fillets in the wine for 3-4 hours. Then place the fillets in a buttered ovenproof dish with the marinade, and cover with the mayonnaise and yoghurt previously mixed together. Top with the breadcrumbs mixed with the chopped spring onions.

Place in a hot oven 230°C/450°F/gas mark 8 for 15 minutes and serve decorated with a sprinkling of paprika.

Scallops with Leeks and Coriander

Scallops are at their best from December to March. Although 24 scallops will be quite expensive, the superb flavour is not diluted by adding other tastes to pad it out. There is no waste and the dish is prepared and cooked in less than 10 minutes. Halve the ingredients to make an elegant starter.

For 4

24 scallops, cleaned and sliced in half
450 g/1 lb leeks, washed and cut into 6 mm/$^1/_4$ inch slices
juice of a lemon
1 tablespoon coriander chopped
olive oil
ground black pepper

Fry the leeks in the olive oil in a frying pan on a medium heat for 2-3 minutes, until beginning to soften. Add the scallops and fry until they start to colour and become soft. Add the lemon juice, ground black pepper and chopped coriander to the scallop juices, and heat through. Serve with good bread or new potatoes.

Red, White and Green Scallops

This is a wonderfully fresh and colourful dish, and takes no time at all to prepare and cook. Asparagus makes it rather special, but another green vegetable such as fresh peas or French beans is just as nice – perfect food for a summer's evening.

For 4

24 scallops, cleaned and sliced in half
225 g/8 oz cherry tomatoes
1 large onion roughly chopped
1 red pepper chopped finely
225 g/8 oz chopped asparagus, peas *or*
    French beans, already lightly cooked
olive oil
1 glass white wine
2 tablespoons chopped coriander or parsley

Gently fry the onion and the red pepper, and when they are just beginning to soften and colour add the tomatoes. When they start to soften – as the skins split, press to allow some of the juice to escape – add the scallops and cook gently for a minute, then add the wine and asparagus. Cook until the scallops are soft and add the coriander or parsley.

Serve with rice flavoured by cooking with 2 quarters of a lemon in the water.

Seafood with Mustard and Cream

This recipe is a homage to Rick Stein who has done so much to promote fish and fish cookery over the years. It is based on his seafood thermidor, an early recipe much loved by those who went to his restaurant – although made simpler for this book.

The original recipe is in *English Seafood Cookery* (Penguin, 1988) by 'Richard' Stein!

For 4

450 g/1 lb assorted filleted white fish – it does not matter what fish except that there needs to be a variety of textures
4 scallops cut in half
110 g/4 oz cooked shelled prawns
110 g/4 oz button mushrooms halved
1 leek sliced thinly
butter
$^1/_2$ glass white wine
juice of $^1/_2$ lemon
275 ml/10 fl oz double cream
$^1/_2$ tablespoon English mustard powder
1 heaped tablespoon grated Parmesan
1 tablespoon parsley chopped

Place the leek, mushrooms, fish and scallops in a buttered oven-proof dish with the white wine and the lemon juice. Bake in a hot oven 230°C/450°F/gas mark 8 for 8 minutes and then drain off the liquid.

Add the prawns and then pour over the cream and the mustard powder mixed together. Sprinkle the Parmesan across the top and return to the oven for a further 5 minutes until the fish is cooked and the cream bubbling. Decorate with the parsley before serving. New potatoes and spinach are excellent with this dish.

Megrim Sole
with Clotted Cream and Chives

Megrim is a sole which is caught a great deal in the West Country and is as delicious as lemon sole. Sadly it remains unappreciated by many and much of it is exported.

For 4

4 megrim sole filleted
110g/4oz clotted cream
2 tablespoons chopped chives
1 oz butter
coarse sea salt and ground black pepper
1/4 teaspoon paprika

Butter an ovenproof dish that will hold all 4 fish in one layer. Spread the clotted cream and the chives between the fillets of each fish. Dot the top of the fish with a little butter and the salt and pepper to taste.

Bake in a hot oven 230°C/450°F/gas mark 8 for 10 minutes. Dust with paprika to decorate, and serve.

Spinach and new potatoes go well with the megrim.

Torbay Sole
stuffed with Crab and Prawns

Torbay sole is lovely and yet is often shunned simply because it is less well known – in fact its name has been changed from witch sole in an effort to make it more popular. It tastes every bit as good as lemon sole and can be fatter with denser flesh.

For 4

4 small or 2 large Torbay soles filleted
20 prawns
225 g/8 oz mixed crabmeat
225 ml/8 fl oz double cream
juice of 2 lemons
2 tablespoons chives chopped
sea salt and ground black pepper to taste

Cut the prawns in half and mix with the crabmeat, most of the chives and the double cream – this is the stuffing mixture. Pour a little of the lemon juice into an ovenproof dish. If the fillets are small, first lay down the bottom fillet, placing some stuffing on top and then covering with the other fillet. If they are large soles, the fillets will need to be cut lengthways before stuffing them in the same manner.

Add sea salt and ground black pepper to taste and cover with the remainder of the lemon juice – you will have to use your judgement: if the lemons are large you may not need to use all the juice.

Place in a hot oven 230°C/450°F/gas mark 8 for 15-20 minutes depending on the thickness of the sole – check after 15 to be on the safe side. Decorate with the remainder of the chives.

Squid with Garlic, Coriander and Olives

Squid (and octopus) look somewhat scary to prepare but fish-mongers are only too willing to do the tricky work for you. It is fished all the year but is best in winter. It is much more popular than it used to be, but much of the catch is still exported. This is a very quick and simple dish which has a flavour full of the sunny south.

For 4

350 g/12 oz squid sliced
1 medium onion finely chopped
2 cloves garlic chopped
2 tablespoons coriander chopped
12 green olives pitted and roughly chopped
2 tablespoons sherry or white wine
olive oil

Put a little olive oil in a frying pan and add the onion and garlic, cooking until soft. Add the squid and fry quickly for 2 minutes over a hot flame, turning constantly. Add the olives and the coriander and white wine. Mix together over the flame and serve straight away with plain boiled rice decorated with 1 tablespoon of pine nuts.

Hot Squid Salad

Hot salads are always fun to do – they are instant food with the delight of the hot ingredients and dressing.

For 4

350 g/12 oz squid roughly sliced
4 spring onions
225 g/8 oz tomatoes cut into chunks
10 cm/4 in piece of cucumber in chunks
1 cabbage lettuce or assorted salad leaves
12 black olives pitted
2 tablespoons assorted chopped herbs
12 seedless grapes cut in half
4 tablespoons olive oil
1 tablespoon white wine vinegar
coarse sea salt and ground black pepper to taste

Firstly assemble the salad in a large bowl.

Place some of the olive oil in a frying pan and over a high heat fry the octopus for 2 minutes. Add the rest of the olive oil and warm it through, then add the wine vinegar – be careful: it will hiss and steam and make your eyes water!

Pour the squid and dressing over the salad ingredients, add salt and ground black pepper to taste, and mix the salad thoroughly so that the lettuce begins to wilt in the heat and all the ingredients are thoroughly mixed.

Serve immediately with warm French bread.

Tuna and Coriander, Lemon and White Wine

Tuna is caught 3-4 weeks a year out of Newlyn but is always readily available on supermarket fish stalls. Although expensive, tuna is very filling, so the portions can be quite small.

It is straightforward to cook and versatile – it looks like pale meat and can be treated very like fillet steak. It is important not to overcook it.

For 4

4 x 75 g / 3 oz slices of tuna not more than 12 mm / $1/2$ inch thick
juice of 1 lemon
$1/2$ glass white wine
olive oil
2 tablespoons chopped coriander
2 cloves garlic chopped

Cover the base of an ovenproof dish with a little olive oil, place the tuna slices in the dish and cover with the rest of the ingredients. Bake in a hot oven 230°C / 450°F / gas mark 8 for 10-15 minutes and serve with new potatoes and courgettes.

Tuna Stew

This is a reminder of holidays in sunnier climes – tuna is readily available in Spain, Portugal and Southern France, and because of its meat-like qualities lends itself to being stewed with Mediterranean vegetables. The French parsley is used here because of the hint of celery in the chopped stalks.

For 4

350 g/12 oz tuna cut into large chunks
1 medium onion roughly chopped
$^{1}/_{2}$ red pepper roughly chopped
$^{1}/_{2}$ green pepper roughly chopped
1 medium courgette roughly chopped
1 x 400 g/14 oz tin chopped tomatoes
2 teaspoons tomato purée
$^{1}/_{4}$ teaspoon dried oregano
olive oil
coarse sea salt and ground black pepper to taste
1 tablespoon chopped French parsley

Fry all the vegetables in a little olive oil in an ovenproof casserole over a medium heat. When they are beginning to soften add the tomato purée, tinned tomatoes, oregano, salt and pepper to taste, and lastly the tuna.

Mix gently together and place in a medium oven 180°C/350°F/gas mark 4 for about 30 minutes or until the vegetables and tuna are cooked through. Sprinkle the chopped parsley on top and serve with plain boiled rice or couscous.

Sardine with Mustard and Cider

Sardines are in fact young pilchards and are caught off the Devon and Cornwall coasts in late summer. It is wonderful to see such shiny fresh fish. Sardines, as we prefer to call them (pilchards for us are tinned in tomato sauce), hardly need any preparation at all, simply gutting. If you can't cope with the bones, get them de-boned but remaining in one piece. They are excellent simply grilled on the barbecue, but they can also be cooked in more exotic ways.

For 4

12 de-boned sardines
3 tablespoons coarse grained mustard
olive oil
225 ml / 8 fl oz cider

Place the sardines in an oiled ovenproof dish.

Smear each one outside and inside with the mustard and then pour enough cider into the dish to come halfway up the sardines. Bake in a hot oven 230°C / 450°F / gas mark 8 for 10 minutes. You may need to top up the cider halfway through the cooking time.

Serve with new potatoes and a green vegetable such as courgettes or spinach.

Sardine Pasty

This recipe derives from a cross between 'Star-gazy Pie', which is a traditional Cornish recipe made with whole pilchards sticking out of a pie (rather an unsavoury idea to my mind), and that other traditional Cornish dish – the pasty.

For 4

450 g / 1 lb defrosted frozen puff pastry
4 sardines filleted
1 onion chopped
butter
225 g / 8 oz cooked potato chopped small
4 rashers bacon cooked and chopped
1 tablespoon chives chopped
1 tablespoon parsley chopped
275 ml / 10 fl oz clotted cream
milk

First fry the onion in butter to soften and then mix it with all the other ingredients except the sardines and the pastry. Roll out the puff pastry and cut into 4 x 18 cm / 7 in diameter circles. Place a filleted sardine across the centre of each and then divide the mixture between them.

Damp the edges of the pastry with milk and pinch or crimp the edges together carefully so that none of the precious juices can escape.

Glaze with milk and place in a medium oven 180°C / 350°F / gas mark 4 for 30 minutes until the pasty is a golden brown.

Stuffed Sardines

Sardines are such a versatile fish, full of flavour. They are caught in the South-west during the summer when they are plentiful and cheap. Once de-headed, gutted and de-boned, but still remaining in one piece, they lend themselves very well to stuffing. Almost anything will taste good – be inventive!

For 4

12 sardines de-boned

For mushroom stuffing
6 salted sardine fillets or anchovies roughly chopped
110g/4oz mushrooms roughly chopped
1 small onion roughly chopped
1 teaspoon dried oregano
1 tablespoon tomato purée
olive oil
ground black pepper to taste

Fry the onion and the mushrooms in a little olive oil until softened. Add the remainder of the ingredients, mix and then stuff the sardines. Place in an ovenproof dish and bake in a hot oven 230°C/450°F/gas mark 8 for 10 minutes. Serve with lemon quarters and salad.

For red pepper stuffing
1 small red onion roughly chopped
1 red pepper roughly chopped
1 tablespoon pine nuts
1 tablespoon sultanas
1 tablespoon tomato purée
1 tablespoon French parsley roughly chopped
olive oil
ground black pepper to taste

Make the stuffing as above. Cook and serve in the same way.

Sea Bass with Fresh Herb Butter

Much of the bass on sale is farmed; fresh wild sea bass is caught in the waters of the South-west. It is at its best between June and February. Unfortunately it is expensive but it is worth buying once in a while, as it is a superb fish and best cooked simply.

For 4

4 fillets sea bass
50 g/2 oz butter softened
1 dessertspoon French parsley
1 dessertspoon chives
1 teaspoon thyme
$^1/_2$ glass white wine or dry sherry
olive oil
coarse sea salt and ground black pepper

Mix the herbs with the softened butter. Place the bass fillets in an ovenproof dish and smear with the butter mixture. Season to taste and pour the wine or sherry around the fish.

Place in a hot oven 230°C/450°F/gas mark 8 for 10 minutes. Watch the cooking time carefully – the fish should only be just done and the butter not burnt.

Serve with some extravagant vegetable such as asparagus or really fresh garden peas. Nothing could be finer.

Turbot in Red Wine

Turbot is one of the kings of fish – it tends to be expensive but is great as a treat. It is caught in the South-west in April, May and June. It is a large fish, so fillets can usually serve more than one person. Red wine is unusual with fish, but I think it works very well.

For 4

4 x 150-175 g/5-6 oz pieces of turbot fillet
plain flour for coating
olive oil
1 glass red wine
1 lemon squeezed
1 small red onion chopped
2 cloves garlic chopped
1 tablespoon chopped parsley
110 g/4 oz mushrooms chopped
coarse sea salt and ground black pepper to taste

Fry the onion, garlic and mushrooms in olive oil until nearly soft. Coat the pieces of fish with flour and fry lightly, turning once. Add the lemon juice, wine, parsley, salt and pepper to taste and simmer for 5 minutes until the fish is tender.

Whiting with Mustard

Whiting is a member of the cod family, but has the advantage of being much cheaper and readily available. It is at its best in the winter and has sweet flesh which flakes. A lovely fish.

For 4

4 whiting fillets
1 glass white wine
4 teaspoons Dijon mustard
1 small red onion chopped
1 tablespoon breadcrumbs
1 tablespoon French parsley
coarse sea salt and ground black pepper to taste
olive oil

In a saucepan bring the wine to the boil with the chopped red onion, the mustard and the chopped parsley. Cook for 3 minutes. Place the whiting fillets in an oiled ovenproof dish and cover with the sauce, topped by the breadcrumbs and salt and pepper to taste. Place in a hot oven 230°C/450°F/gas mark 8 for 10 minutes and serve.

Lobsters, Crabs and Oysters

Lobsters and crabs are very much part of the seafood of the West Country. At harbours all around the coast, small boats can be seen going out to check their pots or returning with their catch and unloading at the harbourside. The trade in shellfish is seasonal and also depends very much on the weather – the boats are small and the gear can get damaged in bad weather. April until October is when most of these shellfish are caught. It is estimated that there are 30,000 lobster pots between Newquay in Cornwall and Hartland Point in Devon – multiply that to take account of the rest of the coastline and a vast industry emerges.

Lobsters and crabs make for wonderful eating – the fishmonger will prepare or 'dress' them for you. There are numerous recipes for them, but I think they are so good that they deserve to be served without embellishment to allow us to savour their fabulous flavours. Mayonnaise, salad and boiled new potatoes are all that is required.

Oysters are farmed in Cornwall at Port Navas on the Helford River and at Fowey. More interestingly between September and April the classic working boats can be seen in Falmouth Bay. Using sail only, they work the shallow banks, dredging for native oysters. To watch the fleet breezing through Carrick Roads is a sight never to be forgotten.

Again, oysters can be cooked – deep fried in batter or added to steak and kidney pie – but nothing is better than eating a fresh, raw oyster out of the shell with a little lemon juice squeezed over it and experiencing that amazing fresh taste of the sea. All it needs as accompaniment is some quality brown bread and butter.

Web sites you may find useful

Several West Country fishmongers have websites and supply fish by mail order, including:

The Pilchard Works, Newlyn 01736 332112
   www.the-pilchard-works.co.uk
M Stevens & Son, fishmongers of St Ives
   www.mstevensandson.com
Cornish Cuisine, Penryn 01326 376244
   www.smokedsalmon.ltd.com

Some other books about local food and drink

Clotted Cream, Carolyn Martin (Tor Mark)

Cornish Cheeses, Caryl Minson (Tor Mark)

Devonshire Cookbook, Margaret Wilson (Bossiney Books)

Farmhouse Cider, Bob Bunker (Bossiney Books)

The Herb Book, Deborah Fowler and Sally Cuckson (Truran)

New Cornish Cookbook, Margaret Wilson (Tor Mark)

The Pasty Book, Hettie Merrick (Tor Mark)

Smuggling Recipes, Carolyn Martin (Bossiney Books)

A Taste of Heligan – Vegetarian and Fruit Recipes, Richard Quested and Paul Dry (Truran)

Vegetarian Recipes from Devon and Cornwall, Margaret Wilson (Bossiney Books)